Escape from Tower One

The True Story of How Vincent Borst Survived the 9/11 Attack on the World Trade Center and Led Others to Safety from the 82nd Floor of the North Tower

Escape from Tower One

The True Story of How Vincent Borst Survived the 9/11 Attack on the World Trade Center and Led Others to Safety from the 82nd Floor of the North Tower

by Marianne Millnamow

Escape from Tower One

Version 2011.8.25

Dedication

This book is dedicated to all the people who are still overwhelmed with emotion, anger, and fear from the attack on the World Trade Center Complex on September 11, 2001. Sometimes family and friends cannot relate to what you personally experienced that day, but there are many people who can, and they are willing to help and comfort you.

I dedicate this book to Vinnie Borst, my friend who saved many lives that day and who is helping me deal with the event by putting my thoughts and anxieties into words. We now will work together in helping others as they move back downtown and reclaim Lower Manhattan. We will "Never Forget."

- Marianne Millnamow

Thanks and acknowledgments

To Vinnie for his endless hours of tapes, telling me his story. To my family, Craig, Jenn and Jason for their support and love. To Tyler and Mary for giving me the encouragement to write this book.

To John Riddle and Eddie Jones for their professional guidance.

To Andrea Merrell and Barbara Kois for their copy and proof editing.

Table of Contents

(Photo by Yann Forget, courtesy of Wikimédia France.)

1

LIFE INTERRUPTED

At 7:30 AM on September 11, 2001, I arrived at my office on the eighty-second floor of the World Trade Center. Although the day began like so many other Tuesdays, I had this nagging feeling, a premonition of . . . what, I didn't know. I booted up my computer and made a fresh pot of coffee, then spent the next few minutes reviewing e-mails in preparation for an 8:30 meeting. During that time of preparation, I reflected upon my years of work within the towering walls of that magnificent building.

In May of 1985, I went to work in the World Trade Center. Employed by thePort Authority of NY & NJ, I assumed my position as design drafts person on the eighty-second floor and began to learn all I could about the World Trade Center. (This was prior to AutoCAD®. All floor plans were drawn by hand on a drafting table with T squares, pencils and triangles.) It was here I learned the importance of office space and interior design. I explored how to inventory existing programs, help groups understand their spacing requirement needs, estimate headcounts, and allocate on paper the square-feet-per-person-per-area for a conference room, meeting area, reception lobby, enclosed offices, and open workstations.

This was prior to modular cubicles. We had freestanding desks, freestanding panels with feet, bookcases, and file cabinets. This presented certain challenges. For example, you could not block the aisles because the panels had feet and protruded into the walking area. You could not put files in the aisles unless there was sufficient space to open the drawers. In that position, with the help of some very knowledgeable people, I learned all about office space planning and design.

Years later when the Port Authority sought to eliminate its rental furniture operation, I met with the staff and inventoried their rental furniture. I drew up a floor plan, categorized it, and generated a list of new furniture that needed to be purchased. I presented my recommendations and we purchased replacement furniture. This gave me an opportunity to grow beyond the role of "Office Space Planner" to project manager. I was able to take a request, have a kickoff meeting with a client, design the space, present a drawing, get sign-off approval, and implement the plan. I managed the electricians, carpenters, carpet layers, porters, and IT personnel. You know, the *fun* stuff. When you take a drawing and see it come to life, it is very rewarding. I worked a lot of overtime to make sure the work done during off hours was performed properly. And, as the rest of America learned on September 11, 2001, vigilance is the bulwark of safety.

During the mid to late eighties, the real estate market thrived and office space in the Trade Center became a hot commodity. This prompted the expedited consolidation of the office space. The Port Authority occupied approximately one million square feet of space on seventeen floors. I served on the committee that developed design standards for cubicles to help reduce square footage. We also oversaw the relocation of the lower zone in North Tower. One such project, the consolidation of the World Trade and Economic Trade Department, shuffled 200 hundred people to the thirty-fifth and thirty-sixth floors. This freed up space on the second and third zones for prospective clients who wanted incredible views of the New York skyline.

That is when I met Marianne Millnamow. In 1989; she managed the furniture installation for the thirty-fifth and thirty-sixth floors. We spent many nights making deliveries, which required the unloading of smaller trucks, bringing the items into the building through the loading docks, and up to the floors. Coordinating the trades and maintaining a schedule was hectic but fun. We learned the structure of the building from the dock and up the different stairwells, navigating paths to make our deliveries easier. From there it was one project after another.

What I learned over those years in Office Space was how life safety and access control go hand in hand with space planning. When you go to a card access system, people want to know that doors are going to open and if smoke detectors are going off, the activation will work and the staff can get in or out in case of an emergency. Cameras and recorders for security were installed. This knowledge would later prove invaluable.

(Photo by Eric Ascalon, courtesy of Wikimédia USA.)

2

THE 1993 WTC CAR BOMBING

In the early nineties, I took a position with the World Trade Department in the Operations Division. They appointed me Operations Supervisor in charge of managing the operation control center in B1 level. My office was located just off the loading dock between North Tower and Tower Two. That is where I learned about the inner workings of the World Trade Center. I now worked within the arteries of the building, moving within corridors unseen by the public. I learned what went on during the off hours with the cleaning crews, more about security personnel, what time the early morning deliveries arrived, how the milk man filled the coolers, and what time the bread man checked in—all the things that made the Windows on the World, the Cafeteria, and the Sky Dive on Floor 44 in North Tower special to those who worked within its walls.

It was an amazing scene to see the security guards rolling out their podiums so they could check people in to the building,

11

watching the porters remove garbage from all 110 floors (just think about the garbage from 110 floors!), and seeing the cleaning people rolling their carts, vacuuming, and cleaning the bathrooms. While the rest of the world slept, the World Trade Center prepared itself for another glorious day. This was my world—this was my working home.

At the World Trade Operations I learned, studied, trained, and came to understand how to handle the contract administration and affiliated operations. Contract administration was the first step in my operation training, along with on-the-job training and classroom instruction. From the operation center I learned the life safety and security piece of the puzzle. In the control center I studied a board showing locations per floor where break glass activations could be triggered. If an individual pulled the alarm, we were alerted in the basement and could communicate with that person and make the announcement to others.

This was the knowledge needed during an emergency. Awareness is key during a disaster, especially learning and understanding the World Trade Center complex, which was a sixteen-acre site with six buildings all connected below with a mall. Below that was the Path Train, subways, storage, and parking facilities. Learning all the entry and exit points and whether they were in the sub grades, the loading docks, the storage facilities below, or the vehicle entry points from West Street, Liberty Street, etc., was mind boggling at times. Sometimes I wonder how I figured it all out. I dealt with landlord responsibilities in an office building in Manhattan, freight elevators, elevator entrapments, elevators that needed repairs, and some that just broke down.

Then there were the off-sites. I can remember going to West Point where operation supervisors learned about interaction with people and what to do in certain situations. I learned what my role was as an operation supervisor, and the roles of others. It was a great seminar that would carry me forward.

Once a fire erupted in the 5WTC Plaza Building. It began as a small trash can fire in an office space of which I was not aware. I walked into the control center during the emergency and saw everyone at work handling the situation. It became difficult to receive a briefing because the supervisor was in constant communication with the responders in the field. I stood and watched, admiring those in charge quickly transform a dangerous situation into a non-event. This calm professionalism would soon be put to the test.

February 26, 1993: The World Trade Center Car Bombing

On February 26, 1993, I drove my wife to a doctor's appointment. My shift didn't begin until 3 PM, but since we both worked in North Tower, I decided to ride in with her and go to work early after her appointment. She took the elevator to the seventy-first floor, and I walked down the block to a Hallmark store to buy my son a gift for his first birthday (a three-foot high Cookie Monster). It was snowing. I asked the cashier for a plastic bag, but she only had paper so I took my purchase directly to my car, which I'd parked in the B2 sublevel. I went through Tower Two to my car, paying little attention to the Ryder Van parked on that level.

I exited the parking garage and proceeded to J&R Music in search of an Eagles' CD. To this day I do not know why I chose the route I did that morning—the Hallmark store, parking level, and music store visit. Had I rearranged any one of them, subsequent events would have been altered.

When I walked out of J&R Music, I noticed smoke coming from North Tower, reaching as high as the mechanical equipment rooms on floors 41 and 42. I ran toward the plaza, pulled open the door, and proceeded downstairs. No one was aware anything was wrong. I opened the doors to the truck docks. Black smoke filled the area. I quickly shut the door and ran toward North Tower. On the way to my office I met a coworker. John and I evacuated the mall, cleared the stores, and worked our way from Two World Trade Center to North Tower, marshalling people out of the buildings.

As I reached One World Trade Center, I met my wife vacating the building. I had to make one of the toughest decisions I've ever made—stay with her or go back inside to assist with the evacuation. I gave her a hug and a kiss, telling her I loved her and my son, Michael, and that I would be okay. One office worker later said the explosion from the truck bomb made it feel as if "a plane had hit the building."

Later that day I came to learn that six of my coworkers from Plant and Structure, who were in a lunchroom adjacent to where the explosion occurred, had been killed.

The car bomb tore through three floors of concrete, scattering ash and debris and sending smoke throughout North Tower and Tower Two. The Operations Control Center, which was located in sublevel B1, was damaged in the explosion. A temporary center was set up on the Concourse near 5 WTC. The Port Authority's critical departments and executive staff were set up in 7WTC in temporary office space.

We'd experienced our first terrorist attack and lost lives, but this live drill proved useful for what was about to come.

(Photo Courtesy of Edward Sarubbi)

(Photo courtesy of iStockPhoto.com)

3

ATTACK ON NORTH TOWER

At 8:46 AM, my boss and I stood gathered just inside a doorway facing north. The sun shown bright, the sky blue. Later I would learn through news accounts the gruesome details of the events leading to that moment of impact.

While our team gathered for a meeting, Mohammed Atta and Abdulaziz Alomari boarded an American Airlines Boeing 767. Fourteen minutes later, at 7:59 AM, American Airlines Flight 11 took off from Boston's Logan International Airport—around the same time that I poured my first cup of coffee and began sorting through my emails.

I was still sorting through emails at 8:13:AM when the pilots of Flight 11 received their last transmission to Boston Air Traffic Control. They were instructed to turn twenty degrees right. Boston air received confirmation, but a few seconds later, when ordered to climb to 35,000 feet, the pilots did not respond. By now two flight attendants had been stabbed and a passenger's throat slashed. Atta and Alomari were in the cockpit. At 8:36 AM, flight attendant Betty Ong reported that Flight 11 tilted on its side, then leveled out. Flight attendant Amy Sweeney called on her phone to say the plane had begun a rapid descent.[1]

Meanwhile, on the eighty-second floor, I joined my boss in the doorway, unaware of the aircraft flying toward us. Moments later an explosion rocked the building. The blast was unlike anything I had ever heard. Instantly the tower began swaying back and forth. Debris fell from the top of the building, plummeting onto the streets below. I had worked in North Tower for seventeen and a half years and the only thing I had ever seen falling from the top of the building was ice. But this was not ice; the building was crumbling.

I rushed towards the exit, preparing to evacuate. There appeared to be a clear path to Stairway C, but the rest of the corridor was filled with smoke—a heavy black fist punching its way into the hallway. The corridor walls had been blown inward by the impact of Flight 11 crashing into the tower. I learned later that the aircraft impacted between the 94th and 98th floors at an approximate speed of 490 miles per hour.

My heart was pumping so hard I could swear I heard it in my ears. I also noticed my breathing increasing. I knew if the others and I were to survive I had to remain calm. I said a silent prayer, took a deep breath, and ran back to where my boss stood gathering the rest of our staff. I shouted over the noise that we had a clear path to stairway C, but *only* if we left immediately. As I looked into the faces of my coworkers I saw fear and desperation. Later, as I recalled that scene in my mind, it seemed like something out of a Hollywood disaster movie; a bewildered crowd too stunned to move.

Escape from Tower One

We headed toward the stairway, still unaware of the fireball ten stories above us. At the time, the corridor remained clear and well lit. As the seconds turned into minutes, some of us began to breathe a sigh of relief. We were making our way down the stairs, one step at a time, and no one was panicking (yet). Our descent seemed to be problem free.

But when we reached the seventy-sixth floor, our evacuation came to a halt. There we encountered what's called a "smoke corridor"— a passageway designed to prevent smoke from the Mechanical Equipment Room (MER) from entering the stairway in the event of a fire. Greg, a Port Authority engineer, attempted to pass through a door, but could not. The door appeared pinned at the top. Greg, a big guy over six feet and about 250–260 pounds, looked at me as if I could do something.

"No sense in me trying," I told him. "If you can't open that door, I'm sure I can't." *We'll have to find another way down and fast,* I thought. Turning around, I led our group back up the steps toward the seventy-seventh floor.

(This image is the work of a sailor, an employee of the U.S. Navy, taken during the course of the person's official duties. As a work of the U.S. federal government, the image is in the public domain.)

4

From the Street Looking Up

Marianne's perspective:

I met Vinnie in the late eighties when I received my first furniture contract for the 4,000 Port Authority workstations. As a small, woman-owned business, I did many things by myself. The deliveries to that building were quite difficult and always occurred at night. During those deliveries, Vinnie showed me all the ins and outs of the buildings: the elevator banks, different stairwells, and how the maze of landings intersected. I think he wanted me to be able to get around easily and safely in North Tower.

So the morning of September 11, 2001, my thoughts turned to Vinnie when from the lobby of a client's office I caught a glimpse of a breaking news story on the television. The news announcer stated that a plane had struck the World Trade Center.

My first thought was, "Well, some poor guy with a new pilot's license just crashed his Piper into the building." But as I

21

stood there listening to the broadcaster's voice shake, I realized it was much more than that and much worse. I bolted to the elevator and out the back door, exiting onto Lexington Avenue. I jumped on the number 6 train but the subway crawled. At the Brooklyn Bridge station, they announced the train was being terminated. I proceeded up the stairs and started walking south on Broadway.

Then I saw it. Flames erupted from North Tower, engulfing the upper floors. A halo of coal-black smoke encircled the building. Instantly I thought of my friends on floor eighty-two. Where were Patti, Mingy, and the rest of my friends from the Port Authority? I was frantically trying to count the floors to see if the fire had reached Vinnie's floor. My phone didn't work but the Nextel radio did.

"Billy, this is Marianne. You there?"

"Mar, what's up?"

"Billy, if we have any of our people in the Trade Center, get them out now! Don't ask questions, just do it!"

I radioed my husband next. "Craig, make sure Jenny is safe. Let her know I'm okay."

"Honey, calm down, what is going on?"

"Where's Tom O'Neil? Is Carol next door?"

"I don't—"

"Tell Carol to get Tom out of the building! I'm heading to our office. It's bad here. Something's happened. The World Trade Tower is on fire. I have to go."

I rushed into the office and my brother Gary gave me a big

hug. I told him I'd called Craig and he announced a second plane had hit Tower Two.

"Don, our design manager, was sitting in design," Gary said. "He saw a plane go into Tower One, then we saw the second go into Tower Two."

"Oh, my God, where is everybody?" I began to mentally go through our staff and accounted for most, but where was my cousin Melissa? She was dating a fellow in the office named Luis. Had Gary been able to reach him? If not, had he heard from Melissa? My heart raced. The girls in the office were hysterical. They told me I had to talk to Teresa, our accounting administrator. Her husband worked for the Port Authority and was in the Fire and Safety Division. I keyed my Nextel.

"Marianne, I haven't heard from him," Teresa screamed.

"I'm sure he's fine. He's probably just doing his job. Too busy to answer. Calm down, he'll be fine."

But how could we know, really? And when would we get better answers?

I ran back to the conference room and joined the others huddled around the windows. At first I couldn't believe it. People were actually jumping from the Towers.

"But why, Gary? That's —"

"Marianne, the building is a furnace with all that rocket fuel. It's an inferno."

The horror of what was unfolding sickened me. I couldn't believe I was watching people—my friends, perhaps—committing suicide.

"The Pentagon was just hit," someone shouted from another room.

Gary turned to me. "Marianne, I'm certain of it. This is an act of terrorism." Then he looked at me in a way I'd never seen before. "Marianne, you are the president of the company. In situations like this there can only be one leader. Can you do that? Can you lead?"

Stunned, I said yes. "Okay, what do we do?"

Still worried about Melissa, I said, "Gary, I don't want to die in this building. Gather the staff together here in the conference room right away." When everyone arrived, I explained that Gary and I both felt we'd just witnessed an act of terrorism. I ordered our staff to make preparations to vacate the building.

Teresa yelled, "I am not going anywhere. I have not heard from my husband!"

I walked over to her and put my hands on her shoulders and said firmly, "Your husband is fine. And I know he would want me to keep you safe. That's what I have to do. This is my job. Understand?" She looked at me with her big brown teary eyes and nodded her head.

"Okay everyone, we need to decide where we're going. I'll get us downstairs and then we'll see the best route away from here. Guys, take off your ties and soak them in cold water. Girls, grab whatever scarves and sweaters you have and do the same. I want you all to be able to wrap them around your nose and mouth."

Trying to remain calm, we walked down sixteen flights of stairs. When we reached the lobby, it was packed with people yelling, talking, and crying. Then came a noise like I'd never heard. *What the hell was that?* People ran down the street as they tried to stay ahead of the white wall of smoke rolling toward us. A girl, covered in white ash from head to toe, banged on the door, screaming for us to let her in. She stumbled inside. Her skin was so white it took me a few moments to realize she was an African-American. She explained that one of the Towers had collapsed.

Gary again gave me that look. *Which tower? And could Melissa be inside?* Just then Gary got word from Luis that Melissa was safe. Thank God! But what about Vinnie? Had he gotten out? If anyone could, it would be Vinnie. He'd always be the calm one, the soft-spoken leader.

He knew the Trade Center like the back of his hand.

(This U.S. Navy photo was taken by photographer's mate 2nd Class Jim Watson as a work of the U.S. federal government and is held within the public domain.)

5

Escape from North Tower

I hoped my knowledge of the maze of stairways, doors, and corridors would be enough to save us.

As I, Vincent Borst, entered the Port Authority's Inspector General's office on the seventy-seventh floor, I was shocked to see his staff still sitting at their desks. I grabbed a phone and called my wife, Rosemarie. No answer. I didn't think she would be in yet, as Tuesday was her day to drop off the boys. I looked around the room and saw confusion, turned to my boss, and told him I was going to look for another way down.

By the time we retraced our steps and reached the conference room in the Inspector General's office, it was a little after 9 AM. New reports later confirmed that South Tower collapsed at 9:59 AM. For the moment, however, I couldn't conceive either of the two buildings would fall. How could anyone imagine such a thing could happen?

I remembered an old exit door that had never been removed.

27

Not so much a "hidden" door as an abandoned exit. We had just built storage around it. I opened the door and stepped into the corridor, approached the center of the floor and looked for a clear stairway. When I got to the cross corridor, I found it black with smoke. The corridor wall to my left was gone; I heard and smelled the fuel. It sounded like it was raining inside the shaft, and as I turned the corner, I saw fire—the first flames I'd seen.

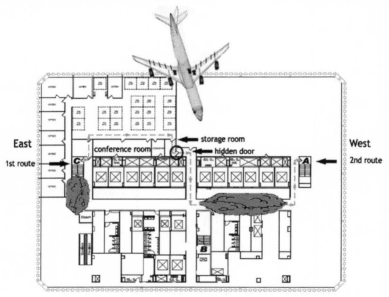

The building seemed to be breathing, inhaling large gulps of air and belching fire as I tried to pass. The flames would explode outward, recede, and roll out again.

After I slipped past the fire, I found two men with hoses trying to extinguish the blaze. I asked them if it was clear to evacuate, and they said it was, through Stairway A. I went back and met up with the others and told my boss it was a bit hairy, but if we went through the abandoned exit and stayed close to the opposite wall, we should make it past the fire.

Escape from Tower One

I volunteered to lead the way and everyone lined up. Before exiting the office, people took paper towels, wetting them and covering their mouths and noses to keep out the smoke. The air was thick. A coworker begged me not to leave her behind; I assured her we'd go as a team. The last thing we needed right now was to have people on the verge of losing it. I returned to the smoke-filled corridor, made a left past the fire again, and asked the two men if they were all right. They assured me they were.

"Keep the area wet," I told them. "We're starting to evacuate again."

I took a position right behind the elevator lobby close to Stairway A. From there I directed the others toward the stairway. Michele, my coworker, seemed to take forever to get into the corridor. I kept yelling, "This way . . . watch the hose."

The valves and rack for the standpipe hose the two men used, extended from the same stairway from which we were evacuating. As the minutes continued to pass, I wondered if we would encounter any other obstacles as we made our escape down the stairs. Our descent put us on the opposite side of the building, but it appeared to be in better shape than the other side. Finally, Michele arrived with another coworker, Patricia, and we began to work our way down.

The stairway was well lit and empty, and we descended quickly. After entering Zone 2, we began to meet with other evacuees. (The building was designed in three separate sections, like three separate buildings stacked on top of each other. Zone 2 was the middle of the building.) When we reached the seventieth or seventy-first floor, we found the stairway congested with others fleeing the building. Everyone remained calm. At every level I would pause and check the floor from the stairway to ensure that no one was left behind. Then we would proceed.

On our two-way radios, my boss called me to ask my location. I had not seen him since the seventy-seventh floor. "I'm on the sixty-second floor," I radioed back. "In stairway A."

He said he was in stairway B, in the middle of the building. I decided we should cross over and as we did, I caught a glimpse of my sister-in-law, Joanne, and her coworker, Linda. We continued our descent until we reached the twenty-second floor. It was there I learned a second plane had struck Tower Two. At that moment, I knew this was no accident.

Another forty minutes passed before we reached the lobby. By now we'd been traveling down for almost an hour. It took longer than I'd hoped because Fire Department personnel continued to enter and ascend into the building while we were coming down. I have always respected and admired our firefighters, but never more than at that moment.

At 9:59AM South Tower collapsed. I'd just reached the lobby.

Still thinking about my wife and my staff, I looked around at the damage and was shocked by the cracked marble and charred ceiling. As I exited Tower One through the revolving doors I entered the mall area, making my way past the stores, coffee shops, banks, and entrances to the subways and at last, finding a path out. Suddenly I heard a loud noise, unlike anything I'd ever heard. Sprinting away from the deafening roar the police officer assisting in the evacuation ordered me to slow down but when I glanced back at him I saw a horrific black mass rushing our direction. The noise grew louder as the shockwave of wind swept toward us. Pipes burst; the mall flooded, becoming submerged in four inches of water. Running became difficult. I dove into a sales booth built into a column support and secured to the floor. Crawling, I accidently turned into the cloud of black wall of wind. The hurricane-like gusts snatched my ring off my finger and yanked my radio off my belt. I wedged myself between the column and booth and held on as the loud wind pummeled me with debris. Tossed about about like a rag doll, I thought about my family and wondered if I would ever see them again. *Am I going to die? Is this the end?* I could not control my fear or the trembling of my chest.

The more I thought about my wife and boys, the more afraid I became. Staring death in the face I saw my life pass before me. Suddenly the noise and wind stopped, leaving me in total darkness. An eerie feeling crept over me. Then anger building to rage. I decided I wasnt going to let myself be buried alive. Flinging the rubble off me I staggered to my feet. I thought of my location in proximity to the exits and realized I was in front of the PATH escalators. *If I walk to my right, I'll walk toward the bank.*

Feeling my way along in total darkness I made my way toward the escalators. I could taste the air. I could equate it to a bag of cement before you mix it. I felt like someone dumped it on the top of my head, and it just kept coming down on me and all around my body. Later, I found out it was pulverized concrete and everything else that was crushed and disintegrated when Tower Two fell.

I exited the lobby and made my way through the mall area, walking towards Church Street. There I ran into a NYC police officer. The collapse of South Tower had left the mall a wreck and he asked if there was a way out. I told him to go through World Trade Center Five. There he'd find a set of stairs and a double door that led outside. As we approached the stairs, I saw part of the ceiling had collapsed. We had to crawl on our hands and knees to get under it, to get to the stairs that would take us to Vesey Street. As we were trying to get to the stairs, the officer asked if we were moving in the right direction. I assured him we would come to a pair of black double doors. Once we were outside of the rubble, he headed in one direction, I in another.

Vesey Street and the surrounding block was like a scene from a movie. That same powdery substance covered me. The air was so thick with soot, ash, and dust from the collaspe of South Tower that I stumbled into a planter. Rescue vehicles, ambulances, and a fire truck sat parked at odd angles, engines running, horns blaring. The noise became deafening and I staggered off. By this time, the plume from South Tower had dissipated enough so you could make out the surrounding areas.

With my extensive training (as HazMat, First Responder, and with Incident Command training), I asked the agents from the FBI and ATF if they had tested the air quality. I needed to know if they had taken samples of what it was we were breathing. They refused to answer. I guess I got a little agitated. I mean, it was a simple yes or no question. Finally, one of them said, "No," and I thanked him and moved on to the intersection of Church and Vesey streets. You could see the disbelief and confusion. Standing in a mixture of office supplies, papers, documents, pulverized construction debris, and concrete dust, I felt like it was the end of the world. Not knowing what had just occurred and not knowing whether this incident was just the beginning of something worse, it just got to me—especially not knowing where my family was and if I would ever see them again.

I stepped through the broken window pane of the Stage Deli. There an officer lay completely covered in ash. I grabbed as many waters as I could, headed outside, and started handing out the water and telling people to rinse out their mouths and clean off their faces. I moved up Church Street to the north where I ran into a Japanese film crew who asked where I was during the attack. I never saw that entire piece, but clips of it appear in *Voices of 9-11,* which was a documentary by National Geographic.

By now, due to fatigue and shock, I began to lose my sense of direction and time. I turned around and looked at North Tower and started to count from the seventy-eighth floor. The mechanical equipment room was on seventy-five and seventy-six and you could tell it had a raised ventilation fan area. All of a sudden it started to implode. I could not believe what I was seeing. The building—my building—was disintegrating before my eyes. I began running from the plume.

I found a bench by Tribeca Park near Franklin and Church streets, south of the Holland Tunnel, and collapsed. An older woman approached me and asked if she could take my picture. I looked at her and nodded. For a very long time I did not move. Then, slowly, I went to find my family.

(Photo Courtesy of Edward Sarubbi)

6

Rebuilding the Office

I do not think I have mourned the Towers yet. We lost about eighty-four employees who were friends. Perhaps that is why. People matter more than buildings. But there is an emptiness that will always be there, even if they should decide to rebuild the Towers. The structure will be the same. Working in the Towers and designing floor plans was electrifying. I called the Towers "my Manhattan Misfits" because they did not fit; they stood out. I had a personal love for them. I assumed I would be working within their walls until I retired. I was wrong. - Vinnie

In July of 2001, Larry Silverstein Properties leased the World Trade Center Complex and the Port Authority went into the transition mode. We were scheduled to complete this transaction by October of 2001. My role was to maintain the lease within the WTC and manage the space for the Port Authority departments and staff. This is the role I thought would carry me through the end of my career. Obviously, that day in September changed everything.

35

I do not remember a great deal about what took place on the day after the attacks, but I do recall trying to go to work the next day and finding all the main roads closed. I tried to go in through Fort Lee, but hit a detour, got very lost, and returned home. I collapsed on the couch; I guess all the mental and physical emotions from the day before caught up to me. I felt exhausted, not from physical pain, but from the emotional wounds I'd suffered during my escape from North Tower.

On Thursday, I visited my family doctor. Friday, I went to work and set up temporary work spaces for some of the employees. I knew I needed help so I paged my porters. I did this often. They responded immediately, sending three guys to help. For four days following the attacks, all air traffic in the area ceased. The silence seemed eerie, especially having lived for so long near Newark Airport. The quiet accentuated the void in our lives, as if creating an empty cathedral for our silent cries.

In a sense we'd lost the fabric of our freedom. Not completely, but our swagger was gone, emotions on edge. On my drive to work one morning I saw a airliner streaking across the sky, the first since the attack. I pulled off the road, my eyes filled with tears. At that moment, I heard "Little Did She Know (She Kissed a Hero)." Kristy Jackson had recorded the song for the heroes of Flight 93. I sat there and wept.

We had a centralized number we had to call every day for the staff. I remained in contact with my boss and always knew where to report. A week after the attack our director held a staff meeting. Those in the room expressed a lot of fear; others, anger. A coworker came to me after the meeting. We'd escaped together. She said she was physically and emotionally ill. I immediately sent her home. She did not return until several months later.

As the manager of New York Relocations in office space, the

responsibility of finding medium to long term space for the Port Authority fell to me. There would be a three-step process to move the staff back to Manhattan. First, get essential executives and their staff settled into temporary offices. This usually involved six to eight individuals for each department. Second, find room for the remainder of each department, usually twenty to twenty-five people. The final task was to find a space large enough to replace the almost one-million-square-footage-space we'd lost in the collapse of North Tower.

September 17, 2001, I entered 225 Park Avenue South. The space appeared large enough. Shortly thereafter, the Port Authority leased 313,000 square feet. The members of the Port Authority remained scattered, but at least now we had the hope of a home. I promised myself I would not rest until we were united.

I spent my time at a quiet place on 19th Street called Tracy J's. The owner, Art, allowed me to take a few tables and move some lights around so I had a makeshift office. The restroom was in the basement and, having descended those eighty-two floors that fateful day, I struggled to get up and down the steps. Still, I was happy to have a quiet office of my own.

To remember and commiserate the fallen heroes, victims, coworkers, and friends, I spent long nights reviewing magazines, newspapers, and books, trying to understand the events that occurred that day at the World Trade Center. For me the timeline of the attack took on personal meaning.

At 8:14 AM, United Airlines Flight 175 left Logan International bound for Los Angeles International Airport. Six minutes later, American Airlines Flight 77 left Dulles International Airport, also in route to Los Angeles International Airport. Shortly after 8:30 AM, President Bush's motorcade left the Colony Beach and Tennis Resort on Longboat Key and headed to Sarasota, Florida and the Emma E. Booker Elementary School. Finally, at 8:42 AM, United Airlines Flight 93 departed Newark International Airport. Four airplanes, one president, and millions of citizens going about their day . . .yet, lives, careers, and nations changed forever.

The memorials and funerals began.

I paid my respects to those I knew and worked with. The Port lost eighty-four staff members, including contractors and consulting staff. Of those eighty-four, I worked very closely with twenty-two. One in particular, Eddie Strauss, was my closest friend. My eyes were glued to the TV, hoping and praying there was an area down below with survivors. There was not. Unable to say goodbye, I wrote a poem for Eddie. The words came to me on September 22nd at 2:00 A.M. while having drinks and listening to music.

Going On

As it is so hard to believe, it is true.
As real as real can get, nightmares come true.
How hard it is to understand.
As empty it will always be.
Pain so strong, with no sign of relief.
As I go on my heart bleeds badly for you.
As I walk into the next day I will always look back,
To see you, to hear you, to talk to you.

Going on is what has to happen and will.
Going on I must guide my family.
Going on but never forgetting my friend.
As I go on my heart bleeds badly for you.

Escape from Tower One

Pain so strong, with no sign of relief.
The emptiness will always be there.
Going on but never forgetting you, my friend.
Going on and always seeing you.
Going on and always hearing you.
Going on and always looking back
Never forgetting you.
You and your family will always be in my heart and prayers.
God bless you.

Vincent Borst, September 22, 2001

❊ ❊ ❊

Eddie was like a big brother, a mentor. He was a person full of energy and knowledge and was not afraid to share it. His wife held a memorial service for him on October 14, 2001. My wife, sons, sister-in-law, and I drove up from Seaside, New Jersey, to pay our respects. I don't know if the poem went into the coffin or if she still has it, but I want Ed's wife and their son, little Eddie, to know my friend will be missed.

Ed would be pissed if we did not rise above this. I pray we have.

While attending wakes, memorials, and funerals, I became obsessed with collecting anything that pertained to our folks from the Port Authority. I didn't want us to ever forget. I purchased anything that would document the events of that day. I listened as people told me their stories. I gathered historical information, read about how and why the buildings collapsed. The devastation became a part of my life.

The day the Twin Towers collapsed, I lost my babies. I looked up to those Towers, admiring them for what they stood for— soaring capitalism, human success, and symbols of freedom.

They were my first love, and I miss them.

In early October, the Port Authority held a ceremony at Madison Square Garden to allow a time of reflection and remembrance. Those of us in the Port Authority needed to regroup, refocus, and heal. Certain individuals received recognition at the ceremony. I received a medal of bravery for my heroic actions in assisting individuals out of North Tower. I also received a group award for the temporary setup of our space. It was nice to be recognized. The ceremony was very emotional. A lot of people were there whom I had not seen since that day in September. We hugged, kissed, and reminisced. It became an informal family reunion. Even some of the retirees came back. We needed the time of healing.

And still the hole remained—both in our hearts and at the corner of Church and Vesey.

(Photo Courtesy of Edward Sarubbi)

Marianne Millnamow

(Courtesy of Vincent Borst)

7

Ten Years Later

My mission remained to get the PA back to NYC. From June until the end of August, 2002, we worked to move *all* groups into the space on Park Avenue. That September I stood on the corner of Church and Liberty, listening to the names, partaking in the first anniversary of 9/11 and remembering those we lost. One hour from lift off to impact. One day to destroy the buildings I loved. One year to grieve over the innocent, hardworking Americans who never reached home that day.

Each time I stepped off the subway, I smelled smoldering metal and the odor of wet concrete. A viewing stand overlooked the site. I arrived late one afternoon. I'll admit, I stopped to have a few drinks first. I needed to rustle up the nerve to actually go. When I arrived, I found the area smothered with security personnel. I finally made it to the front, overlooking Church Street, and lost it. My Manhattan Misfits, my babies, gone! My heart remained buried beneath the rubble on that site.

Now, ten year later, the way it looks today compared to those early years is amazing. Once the PA took control of the site, I became involved in setting up trailers for the management people. Finally, I was able to do something for those who are no longer here. Slowly the healing began.

My close friend, Bob Schutz, began as a locksmith at North Tower before assuming other duties. We'd been through the '93 bombing and then 9/11. The two of us returned to the site and Bob snapped a picture of me standing next to the last column standing from Tower Two. I could not believe that column remained. I put my hand on it and I felt such a connection, knowing all of those who had perished had a story to tell. I felt such a connection to all that were lost that day. I felt Eddie Strauss. I felt like those we had lost were propping us up so we could carry on. That column became a symbol of the rebuilding that remained.

I stayed active at the site, keeping an eye on all the technical aspects of putting it back together again. This sixteen-acre site and the amount of work required in each corner became mind-boggling. My goal remains to get us back home. Our goal is to move into Four World Trade Center by the end of 2014.

The memorial is amazing.

If you have never visited New York, I urge you to come, if for no other reason than to see the trees planted on the remains. We will activate the fountains during the tenth anniversary memorial. Tower One will have reached the sixtieth floor by then, its branches sprouting above New York's skyline once more. You can see the footprint of Tower Two. The Path Station design is taking shape. All the work on the one and nine Subway is incredible, a top down construction—something I have never seen before. The understructure tying it all together is a well thought out plan. It feels great.

Escape from Tower One

When the time comes to move into Four World Trade Center, we will be ready. When people are faced with a disaster that has the power to take away their spirit, many will let that happen. But not me. It may have taken me awhile, but I am back! I will be happy to be standing on the steps the day Port Authority executives and politicians cut the ribbon. I know it will be very hard for many, but I will be there for my fellow colleagues to help them through. For me it will be the end of a journey that began ten years ago when I stood in the doorway and felt the thud that rocked our nation. I will certainly have a smile on my face.

Shortly after September 11, I wrote a song and I think this will summarize my feelings about moving home.

The title of the song is "Never Break Me."

Ripped from my heart in the worst way
Symbols of freedom and accomplishment
Sheer act of madness and destruction
In a very short time they were gone

My babies I grew to love so much
My babies that once stood so tall
My babies that were so peaceful
My babies reduced to mountains of rubble

You hit them hard, almost knocked me off my feet
But I did not fall
You torched the Center
But I guided them out
They fell on me
But I crawled out
You destroyed them
But you will Never Break Me

45

Going on without them is so unfair
Miss them so, words can't describe
God's got to guide me through this
Time of sadness and emptiness

Bring them back so I can say goodbye
Say goodbye my way
Not this way not the way they were taken from me

You hit them hard, almost knocked me off my feet
But I did not fall
You orched the Center
But I guided them out
They fell on me
But I crawled out
You destroyed them

But you will Never Break Me

I recently visited the exterior hoist of North Tower, stopping on the thirty-ninth floor. From there I switched to an internal hoist to the fifty-fifth floor. The view took my breath away.

There is such a feeling of accomplishment that comes with rebuilding what was destroyed, reclaiming that which was taken. I equate it to your house that burned down and when you go back, there is not anything physically standing there, but there are still all the memories. All the emotions came flooding back to you for it was the place you once called home. This complex remains tethered to my heart. To see this sight now ten years later and what it is evolving into has brought such an excitement back to me. We Americans are a people of progression and progress.

Escape from Tower One

We reflect on our past and push forward. I cannot wait to show you all we have accomplished in these past ten years. The loss remains but sorrow cannot steal the joy in my heart as I reflect upon the spirit that makes us a united people.

Where others kill, we birth dreams. Where others destroy, we build. While others enslave, breed hatred, and teach their young to hate freedom, we embrace those who would harm us. Is this our fatal flaw or the strength of what makes us great? I do not know.

There is one thing of which I am certain. We are still standing tall.

Made in the USA
Middletown, DE
11 September 2021